Crafting with Nature

# INTO THE WOODS

## Science and Craft Projects with Leaves and Trees

By Ruth Owen

Enslow PUBLISHING

Published in 2024 by Enslow Publishing, LLC
2544 Clinton Street
Buffalo, NY 14224



Portions of this work were originally authored by Ruth Owen and published as *Science and Craft Projects with Trees and Leaves.* All new material this edition authored by Ruth Owen.

Produced for Rosen by Ruby Tuesday Books Ltd
Editor for Ruby Tuesday Books Ltd: Mark J. Sachner
Designer: Emma Randall



Manufactured in the United States of America

CPSIA compliance information: Batch #CSENS24: For further information contact
Enslow Publishing LLC, New York, New York at 1-800-398-2504.

Please visit our website, www.enslowpublishing.com. For a free color catalog of all our high-quality books,
call toll free 1-800-398-2504 or fax 1-877-980-4454.

Cataloging-in-Publication Data

Names: Owen, Ruth.
Title: Into the woods: science and craft projects with leaves and trees / Ruth Owen.
Description: New York : Enslow Publishing, 2024. | Series: Crafting with nature | Includes glossary and index.
Identifiers: ISBN 9781978535633 (pbk.) | ISBN 9781978535640 (library bound) | ISBN 9781978535657 (ebook)
Subjects: LCSH: Trees--Juvenile literature. | Leaves--Juvenile literature. | Nature craft--Juvenile literature.
Classification: LCC QK475.8 O94 2024 | DDC 582.16--dc23

Photo Credits:
Cover, 4–5, 6–7, 8 (top), 10–11, 14–15, 18–19, 22–23, 24–25, 26–27 © Shutterstock;
8 (bottom), 9, 12–13, 16–17, 20–21, 28–29 © Ruby Tuesday Books.

# CONTENTS

# THE BIGGEST PLANTS

maple tree

**Our world is home to thousands of different types of trees.**

One way we can tell different trees apart is by looking at the shapes of their leaves.

maple tree leaf

beech tree leaf

pine tree leaves (needles)

oak tree leaf

horse chestnut tree leaf

Giant sequoia trees are the largest, heaviest living things on Earth. The heaviest giant sequoia of all is named the General Sherman Tree. Scientists estimate that this tree weighs over 4 million pounds (1.8 million kg). That's about the same weight as 450 elephants!

## The Oldest Trees

Some types of trees live for hundreds or even thousands of years. The oldest trees on Earth are bristlecone pine trees. Some bristlecone pines are nearly 5,000 years old!

In this book you will find out more fun facts about trees and leaves. There are also six fantastic crafts to make!

# THE MANY PARTS OF A TREE

**A tree has many different parts and they all have important jobs to do.**

The **roots** of most trees grow underground. Roots suck up the water and **nutrients** that a tree needs from the soil. Roots also hold a tree steady and keep it from falling over.

A tree's trunk, or main **stem**, carries water and nutrients to the rest of the tree. The trunk is covered by a tough outer layer of **bark**, which protects the trunk.

Branches grow from the trunk. Small, thin twigs connect to the branches, and leaves grow from the twigs.

## Tree Rings

As a tree gets older, its trunk gets wider. This is because a new layer of wood forms under the tree's bark each year. Inside the tree's trunk, these layers look like rings. You can count the rings to find out a tree's age.

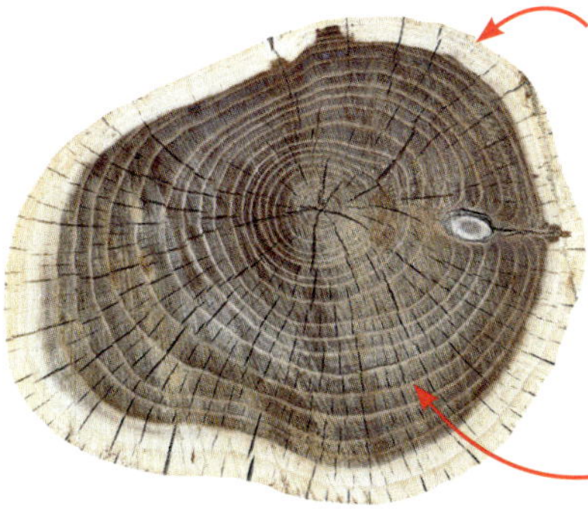

# MAKE BARK PATTERNS

**The bark of every tree is slightly different and has its own pattern. You can create a model of a tree's bark pattern by taking castings.**

**You will need:**

- Trees with interesting bark
- Modeling clay
- Cooking oil
- A strip of cardboard about 1 inch (2.5 cm) wide
- A paper clip
- Plaster of Paris
- A bowl
- Water
- A spoon for mixing
- An adult to be your teammate and go bark hunting with you

## GET CRAFTING:

1. In your yard, at a park, or in a countryside area, find a tree that has very rough bark with an interesting pattern.

2. Using your hands, squeeze and shape a lump of modeling clay so that it is flat and smooth.

3. Press the modeling clay against the tree's bark. Press really hard. You can ask your adult teammate to help press, too!

4 Carefully peel the modeling clay from the bark, and you will see an impression of the bark in the clay.

5 Rub a little cooking oil into the shape in the clay with your fingers.

6 Using the cardboard strip and paper clip, make a little collar, or wall, around the shape.

7 Put some plaster of Paris into the bowl, add some water, and stir. The mixture should be the thickness of pancake batter with no lumps. Keep adding plaster or water until the mix is right.

8 Spoon or pour the mix into the bark pattern in the modeling clay, and then fill the cardboard collar with plaster of Paris.

9 The plaster should set hard in about 30 minutes. Gently touch the plaster to find out if it is dry and hard. If it still feels soft, leave it for another 10 minutes and then try again.

10 When the plaster is hard and dry, gently remove the modeling clay from around the model. You will have a cast of the bark's pattern. Allow to dry for about 3 days. If you wish, you can paint your cast.

# COOKING FOR ENERGY!

**How do trees get the energy they need to grow? They cook up their own sugary food using sunlight.**

Plants make food inside their leaves using water, a **gas** called **carbon dioxide**, and sunlight.

A plant sucks up water with its roots. The water then moves through the plant's stems into its leaves.

The plant also takes in carbon dioxide from the air. Carbon dioxide enters a plant's leaves through **microscopic** holes called stomata. The leaves of a plant also soak up sunlight. Inside its leaves, the plant uses sunlight to turn the water and carbon dioxide into a sugary plant food. This process is called **photosynthesis.**

## Making Oxygen

Humans and other animals need a gas called oxygen to breathe. As plants make food in their leaves by photosynthesis, they also make oxygen. The oxygen comes out of the leaves' stomata. Just think, without plants you would not be able to breathe!

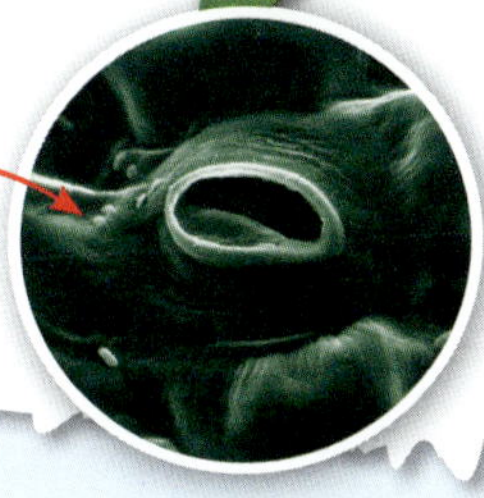


This is a stoma seen through a microscope. It is 800 times bigger than in real life!

# A MINIATURE TWIG RAFT

**A raft is a type of flat boat that is usually made from planks of timber or thin tree trunks that have been bound together. In this project you will make a miniature raft using just a ball of string and some twigs. And it will float!**

## GET CRAFTING:

1. In a backyard, park, or forest collect some twigs to make the base of your raft.

2. You will also need to find a thin twig to use as a mast and some leaves to make sails.

**You will need:**

- Twigs
- Leaves
- String or long grass
- Flowers, leaves for decoration, and pebbles

3. To make the raft, place your twigs alongside each other and then snap off any ends to make them all the same length.

4 Bind the twigs together by winding the string around them. If you don't have any string, you can try this with long, tough stems of grass.

5 To make the mast and sail, use the thin twig like a large sewing needle and poke it through one end of a leaf. Then thread it back through the leaf one or two times.

6 Push the end of the mast between two of the twigs in the base. Your raft is now ready to set sail!

7 Try floating your raft in a sink filled with water. If you are lucky enough to live near a pond, try floating the raft on the pond. Never go near a pond, however, unless an adult is with you.

8 You can decorate your raft with more leaves or flowers. Try loading the raft with small pebbles. How many pebbles can it hold and still stay afloat?

# A LONG WINTER REST

**When autumn comes, some tree leaves turn yellow, orange, red, or brown. Then they fall to the ground. Why?**

In winter, the days are short, with few hours of sunlight. In some places it rains less in winter, too. Also, water in the soil may freeze up and become ice.

These trees have lost their leaves for winter.

With little sunlight and water available during winter, many tree can't make enough food in their leaves by photosynthesis to stay healthy. Also, growing and keeping leaves healthy uses up a lot of energy for a tree. So, in the fall, many trees drop all their leaves to save energy. Then they stop growing and rest until spring.

## Changing Colors

Leaves are green because they contain **chlorophyll**. Plants make chlorophyll in their leaves and use it to make food. When leaves stop making food in fall, they also stop making green chlorophyll. This allows the leaves' other colors, which are normally hidden by green, to show through.

# A LEAF WREATH

**Fall leaves with their beautiful, natural colors are the the perfect material for crafting. Collect some leaves and then turn them into a fall leaf wreath.**

**You will need:**

- Dry fall leaves
- A piece of colorful cardboard 12 inches x 12 inches (30 x 30 cm)
- A dinner plate
- A saucer
- A pencil
- Scissors
- Glue
- A piece of ribbon
- An adult to be your teammate to help with cutting and leaf hunting

## GET CRAFTING:

1. Go leaf hunting in your yard, at the park, or in a forest. Collect as many colorful fall leaves as you can.

2. Before you make your wreath, be sure that the leaves are dry.

3. Place the dinner plate upside down on the cardboard and draw around the plate. Now place the saucer in the center of the circle you have drawn. Draw around the saucer. You should now have a doughnut shape on the cardboard.

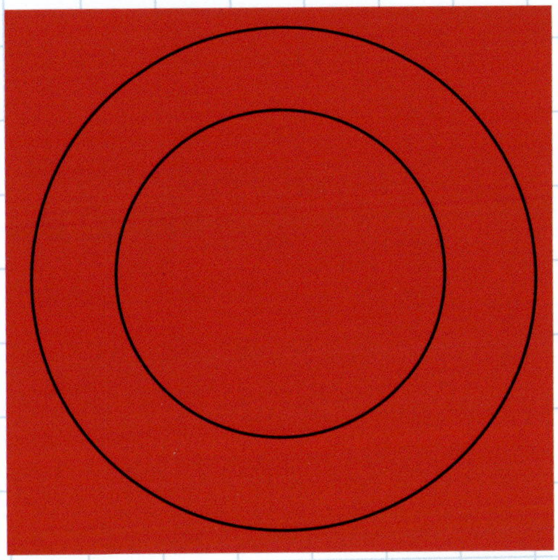

4. Ask an adult to help you cut out the doughnut shape.

5. Now begin gluing the leaves to the doughnut shape. Start by gluing leaves to the outside edge of the doughnut.

6. Next, stick on another layer of leaves just inside the outside edge of the circle, so they overlap the first layer.

7. Keep adding layers until the cardboard doughnut is covered with leaves.

8. Tie the ribbon into a knot and bow and glue the ribbon to the wreath.

# FOREVER GREEN

**Coniferous trees, such as pine trees, are known as evergreen trees. They always look green because they don't drop all their leaves in the fall.**

Evergreen trees lose and regrow small numbers of leaves all year round. Why?

These trees often grow in places where it is very cold and there is not much sunlight or water. Keeping their leaves all year allows coniferous trees to make food whenever they get the chance. This helps them survive in tough **habitats** where it is difficult for plants to make enough food.

Also, growing a whole new set of leaves each spring uses up a lot of energy. So coniferous trees keep their leaves and save their energy!

coniferous trees growing on a mountain slope

## Needles

Many types of coniferous trees have leaves that are known as needles. Each long, thin needle is a single leaf that is able to use water, carbon dioxide, and sunlight to make food for the tree.

# LITTLE PAPER EVERGREENS

**With just some folding and cutting, you can make your own snow-dusted forest of little evergreens.**

**You will need:**

- Thick green construction paper
- Scissors
- A pencil
- Clear tape
- Glue
- Salt
- An adult to be your teammate and help with cutting

## GET CRAFTING:

1. Ask an adult to help you with all the cutting stages of this project.

2. Begin by folding a sheet of construction paper in half. Then cut along the fold.

3. Now put the two pieces of paper together and fold both of them in half.

4. Draw one side of an evergreen tree so that the fold of the paper is in the center of the tree.

5. Now cut along the line that you've drawn. Unfold the paper, and you will have two evergreen trees that have a center fold from the top to the bottom.

6. Now fold each of the trees in half so that the top of the tree meets the bottom.

7. Take one of the trees and cut along the center fold from the bottom of the tree to the halfway fold. Then take the other tree and cut down the center fold from the top to the halfway fold.

8. Slide the two trees together. Then use the tape to stick them together.

9. To add snow, dab some glue on the tree. Sprinkle salt all over the glue. Wait for about five minutes and then shake off any spare salt.

10. You can make lots of these trees. They make a great decoration for winter holidays!

# A HOME FOR WILDLIFE

**An ancient oak tree may be home to 1,000 different kinds of animals!**

Among the branches of an oak tree, robins and blue jays build nests in spring.

In fall, gray squirrels scamper from branch to branch, gathering acorns to eat. Spiders build webs between an oak tree's branches, while caterpillars munch on the tree's leaves.

Look in a hole in an oak tree's trunk, and you might find the home of a raccoon family.

At the bottom of the tree's trunk, its roots disappear into the soil. Foxes, ants, and even snakes make underground homes between the tree's roots.

a spider

a gray squirrel

a snake

## Trees Make Shade

On a hot day, the branches and leaves of a tree create a shady place. People and other animals can get out of the sun and cool off.

# A LEAFY DISGUISE

**Which leaf shape do you like best? Using your favorite type of leaf as inspiration, you can make and decorate a leaf-shaped mask. Here, we've chosen to make a mask in the shape of an oak tree leaf.**

**You will need:**

- Colored cardboard (or white cardboard and paint)
- A tape measure
- A pencil
- Scissors
- Tape
- A wooden stick or tongue depressor
- Decorations, for example pictures from magazines, paper, and colored pens
- An adult to be your teammate and help with cutting and measuring

## GET CRAFTING:

1. Choose a leaf and then decide if you want to make a green summer leaf mask or a colorful fall leaf mask.

2. Ask an adult to measure from the top of your head to your chin. Then measure from side to side on your face.

3. Measure and draw two pencil lines on the cardboard that match the measurements of your face.

4 Now draw your leaf on the cardboard so that the leaf is bigger than the size of your face.

5 Ask an adult to help you cut out the leaf shape.

6 Now hold the leaf up to your face and ask an adult to gently make pencil marks where your eyes are. Then ask the adult to cut two eyeholes in the mask with sharp scissors or a craft knife.

7 Draw veins onto your mask. Veins are the tiny tubes in a leaf that water moves through.

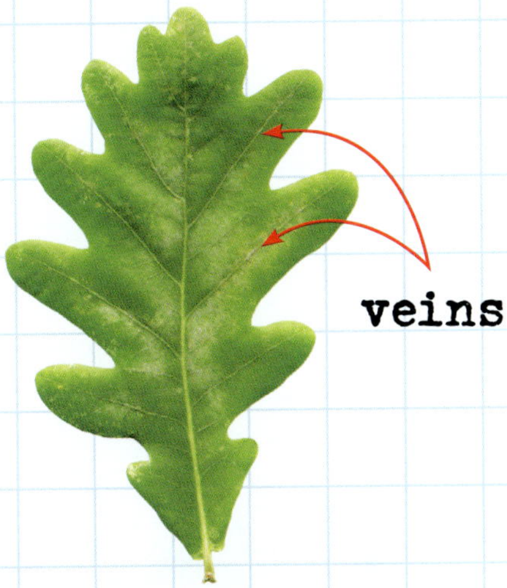


8 Tape the wooden stick to the back of the mask.

9 You can make your leaf mask look beautiful by adding decorations. You can print and cut out pictures of butterflies you find online. You can also draw ladybugs and stick them on, too.

# FANTASTIC FORESTS

**There are many different types of forests. But they all have one thing in common—they are home to lots of trees and other plants.**

A temperate forest is a forest that is warm in summer and cold in winter. Trees, small bushes, ferns, wildflowers, and tiny plants called mosses grow in this type of forest.

Beetles, spiders, birds, squirrels, skunks, deer, and bears are just some of the animals that may live in a temperate forest.

A forest habitat includes living things, such as plants and animals. It also includes nonliving things, such as rocks and the water in streams.

## Tropical Rain Forests

In a tropical rain forest it is hot all year and lots of rain falls. The trees may grow to be over 100 feet (30 m) tall. Butterflies, bats, birds, snakes, and monkeys live in this type of forest.

# A COLLAGE FOREST

**Collage is a way to make pictures using scraps of fabric, paper, leaves, beads—any materials you choose. Have fun making a collage forest!**

**You will need:**

- A large sheet of white paper
- Blue and green paint
- A paintbrush
- Brown paper
- A pencil
- Scissors
- Glue
- Your choice of paper and fabric scraps, beads and buttons, pictures from old magazines, and dried leaves or twigs
- An adult to be your teammate and help with cutting

## GET CRAFTING:

1. Paint green grass and a blue sky on the large sheet of paper to create a background for your collage.

2. Crumple up the brown paper so it looks like rough tree bark.

3. Lay your forearm on the brown paper and spread your fingers wide. Your arm and hand are the trunk and branches of a tree. Ask an adult to draw around your arm and hand with the pencil. Then ask the adult to help you cut out the tree.

4 Make several trees to create your forest. Glue the trees to the background.

5 Decide if your forest will have trees with green leaves or fall leaves. Ask an adult to help you cut out leaves from paper or fabric scraps. You can use beads or buttons, too. Glue the leaves to the trees' branches.

6 Look outside for small dried leaves or twigs to add to your collage. You can add pictures of rocks and animals from old magazines, too!

# GLOSSARY

**bark** (BARK)
The tough, protective outer layer of a tree's trunk and branches.

**carbon dioxide** (KAHR-bun dy-OK-syd)
A clear gas in the air that plants use to make food. When humans and other animals breathe out, they release carbon dioxide into the air.

**chlorophyll** (KLOR-uh-fil)
The substance that gives plants their green color. Leaves use chlorophyll for making food during photosynthesis.

**coniferous** (kah-NIH-fur-us)
Referring to trees that often grow in cold, tough habitats and do not lose their leaves in winter. Many have needlelike leaves.

**gas** (GAS)
Matter, such as carbon dioxide, that is neither a solid nor a liquid.

**habitat** (HA-buh-tat)
The place where an animal or plant normally lives. A habitat may be a backyard, a forest, the ocean, or a pond in a park.

**microscopic** (my-kreh-SKAH-pik)
So small that an object can only be seen through a microscope and not with just a person's eyes.

**nutrients** (NOO-tree-ents)
Substances needed by a plant or animal to help it live and grow. Animals get nutrients, such as vitamins, from their food, while plants get nutrients from the soil.

**photosynthesis** (foh-toh-SIN-thuh-sus)
The process by which plants make food in their leaves using water, carbon dioxide, and sunlight.

**roots** (ROOTS)
Parts of plants that usually grow underground and are used by the plant for taking in water and nutrients from the soil. Roots also hold a plant steady in soil so it doesn't fall over.

**stem** (STEM)
A long, thin part of a plant that connects the roots to the plant's leaves and flowers.

## Websites

**https://rainforests.mongabay.com/**

**https://www.ducksters.com/science/ecosystems/temperate_forest_biome.php**

**https://www.nps.gov/articles/000/all-about-trees-vafo.htm**

Publisher's note to parents and teachers: Our editors have reviewed the websites listed here to make sure they're suitable for students. However, websites may change frequently. Please note that students should always be supervised when they access the internet.

# READ MORE


**Johnson, Rebecca L.** *A Walk in the Boreal Forest (Biomes of North America 2nd Editions)*. Minneapolis, MN: Lerner Publishing, 2021.

**Owen, Ruth.** *Let's Investigate How Trees Grow (Get Started with STEM)*. Minneapolis, MN: Ruby Tuesday Books, 2022.

**Owen, Ruth.** *The Story of Our Tree*. Minneapolis, MN: Ruby Tuesday Books, 2021.


# INDEX